Across An Aqueous Moon: Travels in Autism

poems by

Cynthia J. Patton

Finishing Line Press
Georgetown, Kentucky

Across An Aqueous Moon:
Travels in Autism

ACKNOWLEDGMENTS

Earlier versions of the poems Autistic and My Father's Cheek were published
in the 4th Street Studio's *Saturday Salon Literary Harvest*, 2009 and 2010.
A prior version of Morning Prayer was presented as part of the City of
Livermore's ekphrastic event in 2010, alongside art by Lily Xu.

It has been an honor and a joy birthing this book with Finishing Line Press.
I also want to thank Connie Post for encouraging me to submit a chapbook.
Jennifer Simpson and Monica Garcia read early drafts and provided invaluable
feedback and support. My beautiful, talented, wickedly smart daughter
provided the raw material for these poems. Katie's courage and determination
are a constant source of inspiration. She waited ever-so-patiently while
Mommy completed the "little book," and I'm tremendously grateful for that
along with all the other joys she has brought to my life.

This list would not be complete without mentioning my family, including
Katie's birthparents, and a wealth of amazing friends. My fellow "right
brainers" gave me the courage to attempt this and so much else. I hold you
close to my heart.

Lastly I want to thank Nathan McKenna who read countless drafts, cheerfully
debated word choice, created the beautiful cover art, and even brought me
food when I forgot to eat. He fed Katie too. His unwavering support and love
sustained me through the ups and downs, for which I am deeply grateful.

Publisher: Leah Maines
Editor: Christen Kincaid
Cover Art: Nathan McKenna, 2015
Author Photo: ultra-spective photography
Cover Design: Elizabeth Maines

Printed in the USA on acid-free paper.
Order online: www.finishinglinepress.com
also available on amazon.com

Author inquiries and mail orders:
Finishing Line Press
P. O. Box 1626
Georgetown, Kentucky 40324
U. S. A.

Table of Contents

Dedicated to

Grandpa Jack
who gave me his love of words

and Katie
who inspired them

THIS IS WHAT HAPPENED

An untold wait followed by joyous,
razor-sharp months, then a clear-cut forest
on the blackened slopes of my once verdant heart.
I wandered the moonscape, stumbling over
silence, dragging my grief—an ox at the plow.
Then a stormy angel turned terror inside out,
a seedling sprouted strong and sure
from the debris of my discarded
life.

PIONEERS

I had no idea when nurses lowered
you into shaking, newborn hands
how far we would journey—pioneers
huddled against the howl of wolves.
We followed a weedy, rutted track
into the dark unknown, possessions
abandoned like cast-off toys, bones
hidden in waves of grass, crushed
beneath a fathomless sun. Time peeled
away the others, fear and frustration
swallowed our faltering steps.

Too far to turn back.
Too far to go.

MY FATHER'S CHEEK

Sunlight catches
my father's cheek,
skin like crumpled
paper smoothed flat.

How did this happen?
A tectonic shift in time.
I turned for a moment
and I was the parent
not he.

And yet—
he sits with me after surgery,
puts drops in my swollen eyes,
drives me to the doctor
as if I were a child.

Worries about my bills,
helps prune my trees,
never complains when
his granddaughter
doesn't hug him
for years.

I can count the times
Dad has said he loves me.

And yet—
it's not the words
I will miss
when he is gone.

DIAGNOSIS

The sky cracks, light
skids across a frozen sea.
Words fall, an axe splitting life
forever in two, my soul a glacier
dissolved, a tsunami of senses, fire
birthed in the waning womb of darkness
nearly extinguished, fear consumes.
The doctor talks, yet I cannot hear.
Too much static in my brain—
mirroring the static in yours. I
stand, woozy, suddenly anxious
to leave, cradling my foetal self
and the perfect sphere of pain
that is—this unimagined you.
Outside there is a party in the plaza.
I wander, gripping your slender
wrist, wobbling as I learn
to walk again.

AUTISTIC

Give her back, he says
as if you were branded
with a Scarlet A, his shame
molten glass, spilling onto you.

She's not broken, I say
but he cannot see you as I do—
perfect, whole, unblemished
as I thought he saw us.

As I once thought him.

LOVE

Some days my daughter
shrugs off my touch,
days when we scream,
days when we cry,
days when the weight
of fairy princess panties
must be shed like flayed skin.
I do not hear I love you,
Mommy is a noun, not a name.
I'm pinched more often
than kissed, and yet
I feel loved.

I watch her curled
in a hammock swing,
a marsupial rocking
in a twilight dream and
wonder what the future holds.
Here is what I do know:
it does not take words
or even touch to love—
all it takes is a heart, willing
to be as boundless as the sea.

BROKEN

He chips my shattered
self-esteem: knife-edged
obsidian on alabaster.
There is no high road
in this thicket of despair.
You prance into preschool
and we become pit bulls,
jaws rending the silence,
because I'll tolerate you,
broken you, and not his
soggy, frangible state.
He doesn't understand
this late love is jagged
steel, harsh, unrelenting
like birth tearing me anew,
forged in the fire of faith—
not in God, but in you.

KATIE

You drift through life
Clouds concealing
Sporadic hurricanes
Pass as quickly
As they descend
Part to reveal
Blinding sun
Shadows retreat
All too soon
Creep back
Always a surprise
The surprise a surprise too

NO ONE ASKS FOR AUTISM

He said I didn't sign up for this, as if
he had a choice; no one asks for autism
(or adoption—not at first).
Stole everything there was to steal,
      left me
a broken-down house with a broken-down
yard, broken-down dog, non-existent job.
Didn't mention the taciturn toddler once
called daughter. Claims he was generous,
refused to compromise. Still, I cannot regret
this flawed, fractured man: gained a child
and a career, woke from a sleepless forty-year
slumber. This twisted, treacherous trek—
one I would travel again (and again)
just for the joy of hearing
      Mommy.

LATER

Later, you struggle to say what you want
to eat, pinch me—hard—as frustration grows.
You gather liquid letters that flow through
frantic, feckless fingers, the words ephemeral
      —fistfuls of fog.
I bite my lip to halt the torrent, silver tongue
worthless. Withholding food is tough love
at its toughest, but I'll pay any price.
You cannot afford the alternative.

THE TASTE OF BITTER FRUIT

When doctors said autism my husband wasn't there,
didn't recognize the sour tang of bitter fruit.

Sleepless nights pondering what had rotted at his core:
scattered seeds, bruised flesh, an overripe odor of grief.

Friends pitied my jagged journey: eight-year ache,
lightning storm of loss. Clotted clouds passed through

the gnarled orchard. What he rejected, I embraced.
You are my north star, leading me on a path

unplanned and unpredicted
          —sweeter than the sweetest peaches and plums.

MORNING PRAYER

I'm still in bed as you pass
my room, heading for the stairs.
Can't help but hold my breath
waiting, still waiting, for the day
the words break free, flooding
fallow fields.

You glide past, a shadow
receding with the dawn
the whisper of a heartbeat
tethering you to this home,
these stairs, your world
hidden from prying fingers,

unsubstantial as a cloud.
I would follow if I could
part the mists of fear and doubt,
tunnel into angry tissue,
burrow into exhausted brain,
tie a frayed neuron around

your slender waist and pull,
and pull, and pull, until I
yanked you, tore you
limb by clawing limb
into this world
        —my world.

But how would I
ever know what this
well-intentioned violence
cost you? What pieces
would be left behind floating
weightless in the shadows?

SAILING LESSONS

Your world is a stormy midnight punctuated
by clockwork thunder, an ocean of mountainous
waves to navigate in an unreliable vessel:
splintery deck,
        slippery words,
                unsteady helm.
Each day you prepare for battle—
and I can do nothing but watch
half proud, half scared
while my beautiful warrior
sets sail.

AT THE PARK

You jump near the play structure, silent and shunned,
a pale crescent eclipsed by so many white-hot suns,
flapping and flinching as I patch threadbare tears.
It's easier with adults. You tug a sleeve or hug a hip,

laugh at the joy of connection. Here you are a solitary
moon lost in a chaotic cosmos. Children spurn
your intrepid ventures—a stilted phrase, an outstretched
hand, desire so bald and blistered I burn at the sight.

You jump near the play structure, a universe apart,
timid in your tenuous trajectory. Vibrating, vincible,
as realization dawns that yours may be a lonely orbit—
oort cloud outcast, forever floating the frigid fringe.

Such manifest moments of pain less painful
than the inevitable pain to come.

BE STRONG

Be strong, my mother said
or maybe it was her mom
or neither said the words
only showed it—be strong.

So I worked at getting tough,
chose jobs that required it,
made myself impenetrable—
black-flecked granite, tempered steel.

Thunder came and storms.
I sealed cracks, stuffed what
I most wanted to forget
down the well of my heart.

Tears filled the empty spaces,
breached my dams and levies,
wound their way to tender places
I'd tried to forget.

Until I simply—cracked,
stepped into a new life,
a place where milk and bread are bad,
words more precious than diamonds.

I am no longer stone, but water.
I polish rock and change its color,
carve through mountains, split
them in two, and when obstructed

will create a new path
        and another
                and another
until I find my route to the sea.

THE SWING

You strike the trampoline with the frenetic
force of pulsating atoms, rebounding higher
with each battering bounce, move to a therapy ball
and later a swing, pumping hard and fast—furious arc
etched on a dome of blue, so high that children stop
and stare.

No words needed for that.

PERFECT FALL DAY

One perfect fall day at the zoo. Shiny new
boyfriend in tow, working hard to charm me,
charm you, and you working harder to fit in,
to talk, make him stay. (Please stay.)

Giraffes amble and lions snore; the gibbons
don't hold your attention. We eat sparse, tepid
tacos as warthogs dig, giggle as otters frolic.
You ride the tiny tiger roller coaster

with him instead of me. I smile through the sting.
We have time for one more: Airplane, you say,
face full of conviction. Don't you want your
favorite, the sky chair? (I do.)

You do not waiver as you ride, content to sit
passenger while another child steers. When
the sky chair's shadow falls across our path,
I sigh, repeat your choice. Teetering, then

tumbling headfirst into tantrum. The boyfriend
balks, a skittish horse. It's thermonuclear meltdown,
the worst in years—a test you will not repeat.
The crowd parts as I drag you

screaming to the car, silent drive to his house
punctuated by your shuddering breath.
Afterward I cry; you mumble sorry. We're both
surprised when he calls. At first it's fine,

then crazy at work. Later, he's not sure
he can parent an autistic child, he never knows
what to do. Neither do I. You're different.
I shake my head and he says, you are.

We never break up, but we never date again either.
Eventually I see other men, another subject
we don't discuss. Now I wonder, would things
have turned out differently if

that perfect fall day had stayed a little more
perfect? Or perhaps that flawed and fragile
date was my final pavane
with paltry perfection.

BATHTIME

You slide in the tub for silent stretches, push your head
under so only your nose peeks out, listen to lyrics
in liquid lapping. My love is a song I long to sing;
instead I sway quietly, watching you float swathed in

strawberry-scented steam. One night you hum; I peel
the tune from my brain, store it in a black lacquered
box labeled Katie while you drift in tepid water.
Galaxies swirl behind pale grey eyes.

What stars are birthed in those slippery, silvery hours?

A REFLECTION ON GRATITUDE

The woman from the school tells me to be glad—
    you talk. Other parents covet what I possess.
Brazen indignation burns as slow-witted shame
    slithers down my darkened spine.
You talk—a bit—and I'm grateful, so terribly grateful,
    for that small mercy, but is it wrong to thirst for more?
I want words bubbling over and spilling onto the floor,
    filling me up, filling you up.
I want to know the contents of your skull the way I know
    my garden, still finding blossoms I never realized I had.
I want what so many take for granted—a simple conversation,
    a joke that falls flat, an argument over nothing.
Every time you say something new, I throw a party in my head
    the next moment guilty remembering all you didn't say,
all you struggle to express. I can't reconcile these twin impulses—
    half Mardi Gras, half somber wake—
yet life is sweeter when paired with the bitter.
    Even when I grasp for more, I am graced with you.

YOU USED TO HATE THE OCEAN

You used to hate the ocean,
shuddered at the sound of it;
now you love nothing better
than to gaze at sun-dappled
water, to fall asleep lulled
by the roar of restless waves.
This change gnaws at me, a dog
worrying a bone. I bury it, only
to dig it up and start anew.
I am haunted by the mystery of you.

ONE SPECIAL CHILD

How to express the joy of finding that child, that one
special child, who sees past the headphones and lack of eye
contact, who ignores the flapping and maniacal laughter, who
doesn't care if she repeats whatever he says, a digital recorder

on delay. How to express the gratitude, the wonder, the freaking
awesomeness of a child willing to make the effort—and yes,
it's effort—to play with my daughter, to help her learn what he
instinctively knows. How to express how rare, how utterly essential

these priceless acts of kindness. What alignment of stars, what
combination of traits, what alchemy creates such a child? I try
to explain and he shrugs. Why value connection when you have
never known its lack? I have no words except a meager, heartfelt

thanks.

THE SECRET GARDEN

Your mind is a secret garden, hidden
behind thick, smooth walls. It's filled
with lush blooms, exotic plants, trees
bent under the weight of ripe fruit.
I thought if I waited, the door would
one day open. But now it occurs to me:
what if there is no key? Or worse,
no door? Is it enough to know there's
a garden inside, just out of reach?

LEFTOVER LOVE

He said I thought it would be difficult
to love an autistic child. Indignation
sizzled—drank hurt as if it were a body
of water. Should have dumped him
but didn't, couldn't leave the next one
either, grew grateful for the crumbs
they tossed my starving heart. Then I
met a man who found my daughter
charming, gobbled us up like cherry pie.
We ate green chili soup, burgers and beer,
spicy Thai dumplings, pastries purchased
on a whim—his leftover love
my favorite meal.

MOON GAZER

He built a telescope to show
how close the stars could be,
to show the moon's cratered
terrain—an austere beauty
both pristine and flawed.
We rotated in our nascent
universe: three planets
shifting, sliding, aligning,
gyres converging, stars igniting.
He focused the eyepiece
with patient precision
as the watchful moon filled us
with languid, luminous love.

HOPE BLOOMS

Hope blooms amidst the grass of doubt.
I scatter seeds of time in the vast tracts
of my mind and watch you grow unbidden
toward your strange, silent sun. What
an unfolding it has been, my wild and
thorny rose, dropping petals one by one
to lead my halting heart through hazy,
unspent rain and fields of golden nettles.
I have dreams enough to litter the endless
sky with stars—enough to carry you
not where I had planned but
wherever you must go.

Cynthia J. Patton is a public interest attorney, autism advocate, consultant, speaker, and founder of the nonprofit organization, Autism A to Z. She attended the University of California, Davis, where she received a BS in Environmental Policy Analysis and Planning with a Minor in English as well as a JD. She was the Editor-in-Chief of *ENVIRONS: The U.C. Davis Environmental Law & Policy Journal*. Prior to autism entering her life, Cynthia worked as an environmental attorney, scientific editor, and advocated on behalf of organizations such as the Sierra Club and Save The Bay.

Cynthia has published nonfiction, poetry, and two books on wetland protection and restoration. She hosts the monthly Whistlestop Writers Open Mic in Livermore, CA, and co-produces and hosts Storied Nights: An Evening of Spoken Word. Her award-winning work has appeared in twelve anthologies, including the best-selling *Chicken Soup for the Soul* series, plus numerous print and online publications as well as her blog, *An Unplanned Life*. Two of her stories have been performed on stage. This is her first poetry collection.

Cynthia teaches writing workshops and is completing a memoir, *My Guardian Angel Sings the Blues*, on her unconventional journey to motherhood. The Northern California native lives with her daughter and an exceedingly rowdy dog and cat. Learn more about her life and work at CynthiaJPatton.com